MW00450328

HANNIBAL

A Walk through History

REEDY PRESS

Copyright © 2022. Reedy Press, LLC
All rights reserved.

Reedy Press
PO Box 5131
St. Louis, MO 63139
www.reedypress.com

No part of this publication may be reproduced or transmitted in any form or by any means, electronic or mechanical, including photocopy, recording, or any information storage and retrieval system, without permission in writing from the publisher.

Permissions may be sought directly from Reedy Press at the above mailing address or via our website at www.reedypress.com.

Cover and Interior Design: Eric Marquard

ISBN: 9781681063249

Printed in the United States
22 23 24 25 26 5 4 3 2 1

All images believed to be in the public domain unless otherwise noted.

We (the publisher and the author) have done our best to provide the most accurate information available when this book was completed. However, we make no warranty, guaranty, or promise about the accuracy, completeness, or currency of the information provided, and we expressly disclaim all warranties, express or implied. Please note that attractions, company names, addresses, websites, and phone numbers are subject to change or closure, and this is outside of our control. We are not responsible for any loss, damage, injury, or inconvenience that may occur due to the use of this book. When exploring new destinations, please do your homework before you go. You are responsible for your own safety and health when using this book.

Table of Contents

COURTESY DAVE AND PAULA HIRNER -
FLYING SQUIRREL AERIAL OPTICS

Introduction

The international acclaim of Hannibal led me to choose it as the destination of this historical walking tour book. My family lived in Vandalia, Missouri, but since there was no hospital there I burst onto the scene at St. Elizabeth's in Hannibal, Missouri. Only years later, working as a tour director, did I realize the resounding fame of Hannibal, Missouri. I am still mesmerized by Hannibal. When Samuel Clemens took the pen name Mark Twain and became America's first celebrity, his stories of Hannibal changed the course of our lives as local citizens and how others view us. Now when I visit a foreign country and am asked for my place of birth, my answer is often greeted with a smile from a customs official whose curriculum included the works of Twain. I find it remarkable that inquiries by international folks about where I live often draws a blank stare when I respond with St. Louis, Missouri. When I go on to say I was born in Hannibal, their eyes light up with recognition.

Don Antoine Soulard, a French mapmaker, named the small tributary off the Mississippi River "Hannibal Creek, after Hannibal the Great of Carthage, foreshadowing the explosion of commerce and historical significance of what was to become "America's Hometown." In 1819 Moses Bates built a cabin at what is now Main and Bird. He officially founded the village and named it after the Hannibal Creek known today as Bear Creek. Two years later Missouri became a state. In 1839 four-year-old Samuel Clemens arrived on the scene with his family from his birthplace of Florida, Missouri. In 1845 Hannibal was incorporated and became a town

Bat Gate at Sodalis Nature Preserve
COURTESY DEA HOOVER

buzzing with merchants, visitors, and entertainment. There would have been no Samuel Clemens writing as Mark Twain without the steamboat era.

Visitors desire to tread the streets of Mark Twain's Hannibal and imagine life as one of his characters. Tourists often choose river cruises because they include a port call in Hannibal. When I spoke about my first book, *STL Scavenger*, at The Mark Twain Boyhood Home & Museum, I shared my work on this book. A local woman asked if I remembered seeing the visitor numbers including their state or country. Since we lived in Audrain County, we took *The Mexico Ledger* rather than the local *Hannibal Courier-Post*, and so I had not seen the numbers she described. I asked around and Megan Rapp, now director of

Mark Twain and
Laura Hawkins Frazer
COURTESY
LIBRARY OF CONGRESS

some clippings for me. Those are what you see at the bottom of the page. I am amazed at the distance visitors traveled to visit the boyhood home of Sam Clemens.

I believe visitors are looking for ways to see and absorb the history around them. In addition to Twain, the stories of immigrants, enslaved people, merchants, and the children who came of age in this town, are revealed in these paths. The most surprising find may be the colonies of Indiana Bats. Gale Rublee, nature educator for Hannibal Parks and Recreation, shared with me the beauty and fun of traversing the trails at Sodalis, an outdoor classroom for students and curious adults. Kirsten Alvey-Mudd, Missouri bat census executive director, discovered the large *Myotis sodalis* population, allowing Quinton Heaton, a Hannibal science teacher and Missouri native, to move his classroom to the preserve annually for the bat census.

Many visiting Hannibal are looking for a guide to see the town as a pedestrian. Others might want to learn more as they train for the Hannibal Cannibal 5K. My hope is this book will spark interest and cause you to tell others about Hannibal. Although not all buildings still stand, I believe the stories are important to tell. You can view historic photos, thanks to photographers and archivists, like Steve Chou, who have saved this visual history to share with future generations. By publishing them, I hope it brings life back to the stories that may have been forgotten or been languishing. Finally, I believe this book will be of interest to those who never visit Hannibal, Missouri. They can vicariously enjoy a stroll around America's Hometown using this as their guide.

tourism in Hannibal, said she used to collect the numbers from the museum entrance records and call them into the paper each month when she worked at the museum. Henry Sweets, Curator of The Mark Twain Boyhood Home & Museum, concurred. I emailed the *Hannibal Courier-Post* and they directed me to the Hannibal Free Public Library. Hallie Yundt Silver said they had the microfilm and she was kind enough to take a photo with her phone. When I arrived at the museum, Henry had found

November report Mark Twain Museum
Dec. 4, 1990

Total visitors 5,592
States represented.....................43
Total foreign countries 22

Foreign countries represented were Argentina, Australia, Austria, Belgium, Belize, Canada, China, Costa Rica, Czechoslovakia, Denmark, Ecuador, England, Germany, Israel, Japan, Malawi, New Zealand, Puerto Rico, Russia, S...
land S...

July visitors M.T. Museum 1988

Number of visitors 24,979
Number of states.........................50
Number of foreign countries..........40

Foreign countries represented were Abu Dhabi, Algeria, Argentina, Australia, Austria, Bahrain, Belgium, Brazil, Canada, Chile, Colombia, Czechoslovakia, Denmark, Dominican Republic, England, Finland, France, Germany, Indonesia, Italy, Japan, Korea, Kuwait, Mexico, Morocco, Netherlands, Panama, Peru, Poland, Puerto Rico, Russia, Scotland, Singapore, Spain, Sweden, Switzerland, Taiwan, Thailand, Tibet, Yugoslavia.

Mark Twain Walk

Mississippi River

Cardiff

Mark Twain Avenue

Cardiff Hill Overlook Park

Hill Street

North 1st Street

Center Street

North Main Street

Rock Street

North Street

North 3rd Street

North 4th Street

North 6th Street

Bird Street

North 3rd Street

Center Street

North Main Street

Broadway

North 7th Street

Central Park

Dulaney Avenue

Broadway Extension

South 7th Street

South 6th Street

South 5th Street

South 4th Street

Church Street

South Main Street

Lyon Street

MO-79

Mark Twain Walk

Samuel Clemens, who later took the pen name Mark Twain, changed the way people across the globe thought of Americans. This path will lead you by sites in downtown Hannibal that are connected with the author's early life and his family, as well as locations that have subsequently adopted his name. Hopefully it will pique your interest in learning more in some places and just having fun in others.

Begin at Main Street near Hill Street.

THE PILASTER HOUSE/ GRANT'S DRUG STORE

325 North Main St.

The Greek Revival-style columns, or pilasters, gave the home its name before it became known as Grant's Drug Store. An actual home to the Clemens family during one of their periods of "straitened circumstances," 1846–1847, it was reportedly diverted to Hannibal from Marion City due to flooding. Sent from Cincinnati as a knockdown, it was reassembled at Hill and Main around 1836. Young Sam saw a man who had been shot on Main Street die on the floor there. This event inspired the scene in *Adventures of Huckleberry Finn* in which Sherburn shoots Boggs. As Boggs expired, a Bible was placed under his head and on his chest. The traumatic event never left Twain's memory. In 1847 John Clemens died of pneumonia returning from Palmyra. Finances required Jane Clemens to move Sam and the other children back to the affordable boyhood home on Hill Street. Today you may enter to see what citizens of the era would have experienced in Dr. Orville Grant's store. The restoration took the building down to the interior timbers, and leveled the entire building before reinforcing the structure.

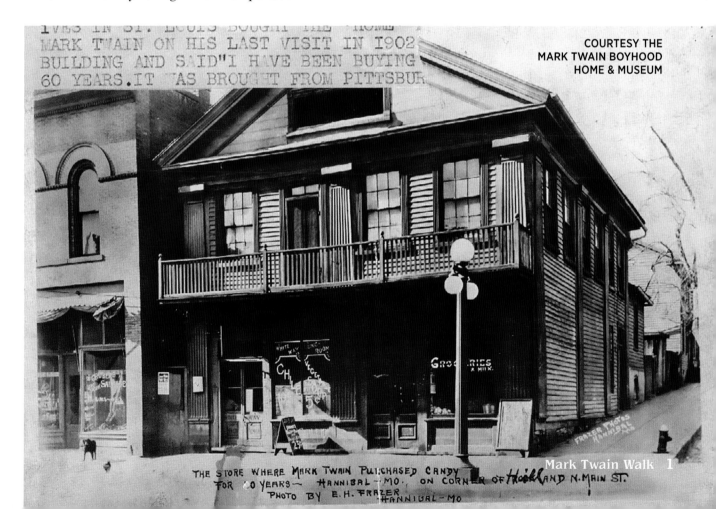

COURTESY THE MARK TWAIN BOYHOOD HOME & MUSEUM

COURTESY
DECLAN RUTAN

Go toward the pedestrian-only area and you will see the Becky Thatcher House on the left.

LAURA HAWKINS/
BECKY THATCHER HOUSE
211 Hill St.
Laura Hawkins was the real-life inspiration for Becky Thatcher, the object of Tom Sawyer's affections. Twain visited her on his returns to Hannibal and they had a lifelong connection. Laura's character lives on, as every year locals choose a Tom and a Becky to represent Hannibal to the world. The white fence near the historic homes brings to mind the whitewashing job Tom persuaded others to perform for him. Every year contestants compete in a fence-painting contest as part of the National Tom Sawyer Days. Finalists must recite a scene from *The Adventures of Tom Sawyer* to be performed when representing Hannibal abroad and in town for local events and festivals.

Across Hill Street see:

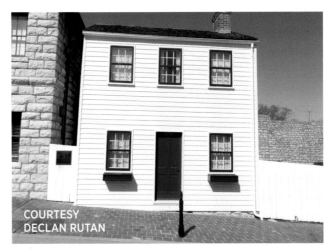

MARK TWAIN BOYHOOD HOME
206 Hill St.
Samuel Clemens's father moved the family to town when Sam was only four years old. This historic event would forever change not only Hannibal but America's portrayal internationally. Sam's father was a judge and often unlucky in business. His mother was a devout Christian woman who was willing to work to get them through their, in her words, "straitened

circumstances." Enter the Interpretive Center to purchase tickets for a tour. Enjoy a step back in time to when Hannibal was still a river town finding its own identity. *marktwainmuseum.org*

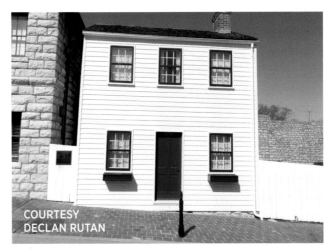

COURTESY
DECLAN RUTAN

Take the sidewalk through the arch in the wall of the Boyhood Home area, go around the building to the parking lot. Look left or west and you will see the Huck Finn Home. Continue to North Street to view it from the front. To enter the home, buy a ticket for the Mark Twain Home experience.

HUCK FINN HOUSE
215 North St.
Here stands a replica of the home occupied by Tom Blankenship, Twain's inspiration for Huckleberry Finn. The original home was torn down in 1911. Pictures were found confirming the structure was a frame house with

COURTESY
DAVE & PAULA HIRNER -
FLYING SQUIRREL AERIAL OPTICS

siding over logs, as described by a workman who demolished it when he was just 13. Museum curator Henry Sweets researched the home of the Blankenships and never found any deeds with their names, leading to the belief that they were renters or perhaps even squatters on the property.

From the front of Huck's house walk toward Third Street toward the Best Western. Continue up 3rd and you will arrive at Jim's Journey.

JIM'S JOURNEY: THE HUCK FINN FREEDOM CENTER (Below)
509 North 3rd St.

Built by former slaves circa 1837 and once a Union Army ammunition storage space, this building now houses Hannibal's first African American museum. Founder Faye Dant strives to tell all sides of the Hannibal story, including that of the enslaved, then the segregated people of color

after the Civil War. Samuel Clemens wrote about the horrors of slavery and used the character Jim to share his opinions in fiction. As a child, Sam met the enslaved Daniel Quarles on his uncle's farm in Florida, Missouri. Clemens married into an abolitionist family and openly shared his views in his writing and in public appearances. *jimsjourney.org*

Retrace your steps to North Street and continue toward the river. Just past the intersection of Main Street look left and up to see the lighthouse.

MARK TWAIN MEMORIAL LIGHTHOUSE
East Rock Street and East Cardiff Lane

A memorial to Mark Twain and his portrayals of Hannibal in his various books, this is the first lighthouse built in 1935. That year would have been Mark Twain's one hundredth birthday. It is located

COURTESY STEVE CHOU

COURTESY THE MARK TWAIN
BOYHOOD HOME & MUSEUM

COURTESY
DECLAN RUTAN

on Cardiff Hill, where Tom, Huck and their gang played. At the top of 244 stairs, the lighthouse was flattened by high winds in 1960. Rebuilt in 1963 and reconstructed in 2019, it is a favorite destination for school groups. Teachers often assign students to count the number of steps and report back. Ah, those clever teachers!

Here at the foot of Main and North Streets see:

TOM AND HUCK STATUE

Intersection of Main St. and North St.
Centerpieces of the beloved adventures in Mark Twain's stories, Tom and Huck are coming back from an expedition, most likely somewhere they shouldn't have been. Tom Blankenship was the inspiration for Huck Finn, and a

replica of his home can be seen inside the Mark Twain Complex. Snap a photo in front of the first statue built in America depicting fictional characters. It was completed in 1926.

Continue away from the statue up Main Street toward Broadway. On your right will be a parking lot with a building set back. This building is the:

PLANTERS BARN THEATER

319 North Main St.
This former stable was constructed in 1849, the era of the California Gold Rush, the cholera epidemic, the *White Cloud* steamboat explosion in St. Louis that destroyed 27 steamboats and 14 blocks of downtown, Elizabeth Blackwell of New York becoming the first female doctor in the US, Harriet Tubman emancipating herself, and the founding of the pharmaceutical company Pfizer.

Notable visitors to the stable included President Lincoln and Samuel Clemens. Still standing where it was initially built to be the stable for the Planters Barn Hotel, the building now houses a theater with performances by Richard Garey of *Mark Twain Himself.* Garey has memorized over seven hours of material taken directly from Mark Twain's writing and performs it without edits or additions. Enjoy a show and be transported back in time. *heritagestage.com*

COURTESY DEA HOOVER

COURTESY DEA HOOVER

Note: Gift shop entrance is free and purchases support this non-profit museum.

Come back to Main Street, turn right and walk for two blocks then cross street to:

⑨ MARK TWAIN MUSEUM GALLERY

120 North Main St.

Built as a department store in 1892, it now houses various updated and eclectic Mark Twain artifacts. See his favorite writing desk and chair, pipe, hat, pocket watch, and $10,000 life-insurance policy. One of the most moving objects is the plaster death mask of Twain's son, Langdon, who died as a toddler. Be sure to visit the second floor housing 15 original oil paintings by Norman Rockwell depicting scenes from *The Adventures of Tom Sawyer* and *Adventures of Huckleberry Finn.*

Continue toward Broadway until you arrive at Center Street. Turn left onto Center Street but note that the boat may change locations based on river level and that the flood walls may be closed.

⑩ CENTER STREET LANDING: MARK TWAIN RIVERBOAT DOCK

100 Center St.

The *Mark Twain Riverboat* began life as the *Huck Finn.* Built in 1964 in Dubuque, Iowa, it was taken to New Orleans. In 1982 Captain Lumpp re-christened her the *Mark Twain.* In 1997, after 18 years of piloting the vessel, Captain Steve and his wife Sandy Terry purchased the vessel, and he continues to regale passengers with stories of the Mighty Mississippi as serene views from

COURTESY DAVE AND PAULA HIRNER -
FLYING SQUIRREL AERIAL OPTICS

COURTESY
DEA HOOVER

the balcony reveal what captivated the young Samuel Clemens and led him to write *Life on the Mississippi. marktwainriverboat.com*

Walk back toward town and turn left on Main Street then right on Church Street. The library will be on your left.

HANNIBAL PUBLIC LIBRARY
200 South 5th St.

Once the site of the Union-supporting Presbyterian Church congregation, the current library building houses countless records and histories both physically and digitally. The first library system in Hannibal was started by Judge John Marshall Clemens (Mark Twain's father), Zachariah Draper, Dr. Hugh Meredith, and Sam Cross as the Hannibal Library Institute in 1845 and lasted until 1870. It was fee based. The next iteration of a library was the Mercantile Library Association, which was formed in 1870 and lasted until 1876. In 1889 the Hannibal Free Public Library opened as the first free public library in the entire state of Missouri.

Helen Garth donated $25,000 to the city to erect this building as a memorial to her late husband, John, an incredibly successful tobacco businessman. Be sure to look up at the engraving of his name along the curve of the library front. An excellent resource for any historian or genealogist, the library can be accessed from anywhere in the world. *hannibal.lib.mo.us*

Continue west on Church Street and then turn right on North Sixth Street.

FIRST PRESBYTERIAN CHURCH
120 North 6th St.

The congregation formed in 1832 and erected the first building in 1839 on 4th Street. Sam Clemens remembers worshiping at the building along the river. Initially enrolled in the Methodist Church Sunday School, his mother and sister later moved all their memberships to the Presbyterian Church. The congregation was divided leading up to and during the Civil War and separated into a North and a South congregation. The two congregations then merged back into one in 1873 in this location. Due to overcrowding this beautiful building replaced the previous building here in 1895 and remains as you see it today. *fpchannibal.org/history*

COURTESY THE MARK TWAIN BOYHOOD HOME & MUSEUM

Turn right on Center Street, then left on north Fifth Street.

 LAURA HAWKINS FRAZER HOUSE

210 North 5th St.

Mark Twain's inspiration for Becky Thatcher was his childhood friend Laura Hawkins. She married Dr. James Frazer and they lived in this 1897 Queen Anne that has recently been restored by the current owners, Nora Creason and Don Metcalf. Their goal is to return it to the way it was when Laura lived here. At age 60, Laura began serving as matron of the Home of the Friendless, which was located at Sixth and North Streets. She served as matron for 28 years and touched many lives at a time when there were no social services or safety nets provided by the government. Laura lived in this house with her son and his wife until her death at age 91. Laura and Sam remained friends through the years, and she even visited him at Stormfield, his home in Reddington, Connecticut.

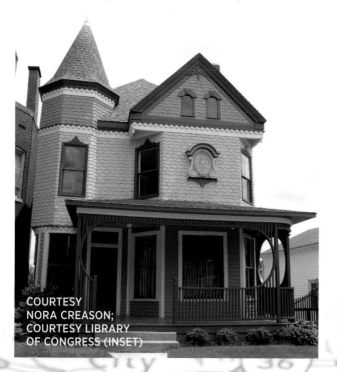

COURTESY NORA CREASON; COURTESY LIBRARY OF CONGRESS (INSET)

COURTESY DEA HOOVER

Come back to Center Street and turn left. Then make a left on Third Street. For a workout, pass Center Street, go to Hill Street, and come straight down to the dinette. Look for the revolving mug!

MARK TWAIN DINETTE AND PADDLEBOX GAMES & GIFTS

400 North Third St.

The Dinette opened with optimism in 1942 at the start of World War II. It has served loose meat sandwiches since the beginning but became a part of the Maid-Rite franchise in the 1960s. Later the Frostop Root Beer franchise became part of the brand; you will spot their revolving mug from various points in downtown. As a young girl, I remember ordering from the Electro-Hop system, which allowed diners to call their orders back to the kitchen. Outside, car hops delivered orders directly to your car complete with tray stands. Today you can still order items from your car at the drive-in including fried green tomatoes and the onion rings are sold by the foot! *marktwaindinette.com*

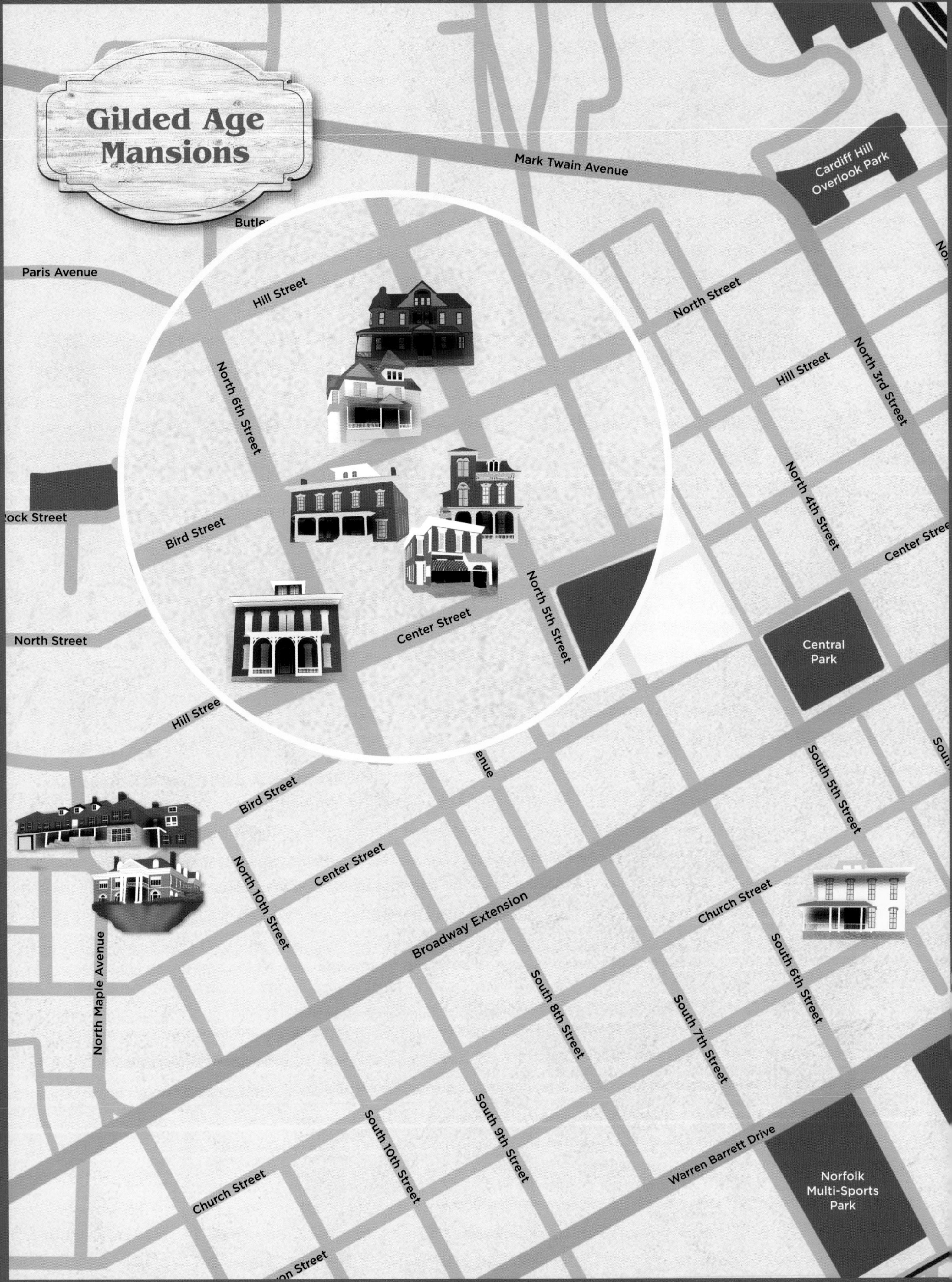

Gilded Age Mansions

Paris Avenue

Mark Twain Avenue

Cardiff Hill Overlook Park

Butler

Hill Street

North Street

North 6th Street

Hill Street

North 3rd Street

North 4th Street

Rock Street

Bird Street

Center Street

North 5th Street

Center Street

North Street

Hill Street

Central Park

Bird Street

South 5th Street

Center Street

North 10th Street

Broadway Extension

Church Street

South 6th Street

South 8th Street

South 7th Street

North Maple Avenue

Church Street

South 9th Street

Warren Barrett Drive

South 10th Street

Norfolk Multi-Sports Park

Gilded Age Mansions

Mark Twain coined the term "The Gilded Age" in the book of the same name. Most of these homes—some bed-and-breakfasts, others private residences—are located along Fifth Street, considered very desirable at the time of construction. Find other homes in the Central Park and Maple Avenue Districts by picking up the maps at the Hannibal Visitors Center.

Begin at Fifth Street between Church and Lyon.

213 South 5th St.
John and Helen Garth, lifelong friends of Sam Clemens since childhood, built this home in 1858. The Italianate Villa with a cupola offering a view of the Mississippi River is located along Millionaire's Row. Helen hosted a dinner here upon Clemens's return in 1902 that included Laura Hawkins, the model for Twain's character Becky Thatcher, as a guest. Clemens and Mrs. Garth visited Mt. Olivet Cemetery to pay respects to her late husband and his parents. In 1910 Mrs. Garth was the first woman elected to the board of the Farmers & Merchants Bank.

COURTESY RICHARD GAREY

COURTESY VISIT HANNIBAL

Head northwest on Fifth Street toward Church Street and continue just past Center Street and look to your left.

LABINNAH BISTRO
207 North 5th St.
What a strange name, right? Well, it is a throwback to the Labinnah Social Club. It was "formed for the promotion and enjoyment of social intercourse, good fellowship, innocent diversion, recreation and amusement." Note that Labinnah is an emordnilap of the name Hannibal. The December 29, 1888 party held in this 1870 home built by W. A. Munger marked the last night of Amos Stillwell's life. He returned to his home to be murdered that night. The crime is still unsolved today.

Continue on Fifth Street toward Bird Street and turn left.

THE BELVEDERE INN
521 Bird St.
Built in 1859 by Alfred Lamb, vice president of the Hannibal and St. Joseph Railroad line, it was later purchased by Lyman P. Munger, of the Hannibal Lime Company. It was referred to as the Lamb–Munger House prior to its restoration by Bob Yapp, one of the country's

COURTESY DEA HOOVER

COURTESY VISIT HANNIBAL

foremost authorities on restoration, and his wife Pat, who runs the operations of the mansion.

Admire the work on the exterior of this amazing mansion and don't forget to look up! The cupola is considered one of the most attractive, if not tallest, in town. Guests will find custom woodwork, painting, and charming decorations selected by Pat and Bob. *belvedereinnhannibal.com*

Head northeast on Bird Street toward Fifth Street.

4

313 North 5th St.

Built in the Queen Anne style in 1889 by lumber baron W. B. Pettibone, this building features 19th century stained glass and exterior woodwork. This can be considered Pettibone's starter home, as it preceded Cliffside, his most grand family home, by 13 years. Mr. Pettibone is responsible for the creation of Riverview Park and was known as a philanthropist in the community. He built the Laura Jones Pettibone Memorial School, which he dedicated to his late wife. It's an amazing restoration that continues the Victorian tradition in Hannibal today.

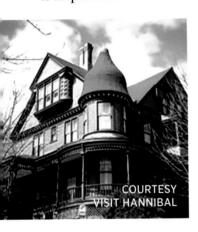

COURTESY VISIT HANNIBAL

Head southeast on Fifth Street.

5

GARDEN HOUSE BED & BREAKFAST

301 North 5th St.

Albert Pettibone, brother of Wilson B. (known as W. B.), another lumber baron, one who inherited the Hannibal Saw Mill Co. and the Hannibal Sash Co., built this home in 1896. Then

COURTESY VISIT HANNIBAL

stove magnate Charles Trowbridge owned the home and later passed it along to his son. The bright colors make this home stand out from the crowd. *gardenhousebedandbreakfast.com*

Head south on North 5th toward Bird St.

6

DUBACH INN, Bed and Breakfast

221 North 5th St.

Swiss lumberman David Dubach built this Mansard-roof villa in the Italianate style in 1871 when the log business was booming. His daughter Jeannie Mae married the founder of the Fette Orchard company. In the family for over 100 years, it is now operated as a bed and breakfast. *dubachinn.com*

COURTESY DUBACH INN

COURTESY DEA HOOVER

Head northwest on Fifth Street and turn left on Bird Street and left on Sixth Street.

7

ROBARDS MANSION

215 North 6th St.

John L. Robards, attorney, lumber baron, and lifelong friend of Samuel Clemens, built this luxurious home in 1871. This Italianate mansion is listed on the National Register of Historic Places in the Central Park Historic

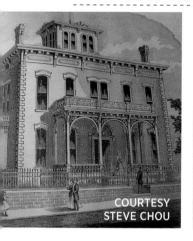

COURTESY
STEVE CHOU

COURTESY
DEA HOOVER

COURTESY
STEVE CHOU

District. Be sure to look up from across the street and see the cupola and the decorative joining spots, known as *quoins*. When Sam returned to Hannibal for the last time in 1902, he visited Robards. Inside is one of only two remaining flying staircases in Hannibal. A flying staircase is built without a central support and considered quite a bragging right. Roman numerals were located under the bannister, most likely sequencing the order of pieces for the reassembly inside this grand home. There are 72 steps up to the cupola. It was the first home in Hannibal to have indoor plumbing. Interestingly, Mark Twain reenactor Richard Garey and his wife Patricia, an artist, recently owned this home and renovated it before lovingly passing it along to the next caretaker. Check out the YouTube video for a tour inside: *youtube/dkWqg19hYek.*

Author's Note: Do not believe Google Maps that the walk is: mostly flat. It is mostly flat except for going up the hills! Whether you drive or walk, don't miss taking a gander at them. It is time well spent.

Head northwest on Sixth Street toward Bird Street and turn left.

ROCKCLIFFE MANSION
1000 Bird St.
In 1902 on his last visit home, Mark Twain spoke to 300 people from the Grand Hall of this mansion built by lumber baron John Cruikshank, Jr. Filled with the most exotic woods, Tiffany windows and chandeliers, Cruikshank wanted a show place with the best that money

could buy. $250,000 later, Rockcliffe was complete. It sat vacant for 43 years, then was saved by three local families. Fortunately, much was left under the accumulated debris. The sturdy architecture held up through the decades of abandonment and vandalism, and it stands restored with much of its original furnishings. Not just owners, but true caretakers have opened the home as a public house museum and also operate it as a bed and breakfast. *rockcliffemansion.com*

Head southwest on Bird Street toward Tenth Street and stay left.

CLIFFSIDE
8 Stillwell Pl.
Designed by George Van Doren Shaw, a contemporary of Frank Lloyd Wright, this beautiful mansion was built for philanthropist and lumber baron W. B. Pettibone in 1912. Situated on two rolling acres, it affords a marvelous view as well as privacy. Mr. Pettibone's philanthropy included donating multiple plots of land for public use, and during the Great Depression he generously secured 3,000 children's savings accounts.

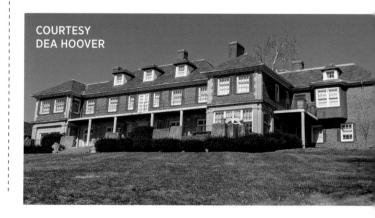

COURTESY
DEA HOOVER

Women of Hannibal

Mississippi River

Pleasant Avenue

Mark Twain Avenue

Paris Avenue

Lincoln Street

Orchard Street

Rock Street

Rock Street

Hill Street

Bird Street

North Street

North 4th Street

North 3rd Street

North Main Street

North 5th Street

North 6th Street

Center Street

Central Park

Church Street

South 4th Street

Grand Avenue

Bird Street

North 10th Street

Broadway Extension

South 5th Street

South 6th Street

South 7th Street

Warren Barrett Drive

Clemens Field

South 8th Street

South 9th Street

Church Street

South 10th Street

Lyon Street

South 11th Street

South Maple Avenue

Colfax Avenue

Norfolk Multi-Sports Park

Broadway Extended

Market Street

Warren Barrett Drive

Dulany Park

Sodalis Park

110

Women of Hannibal

Margaret Tobin Brown (*The Unsinkable Molly Brown*) will forever be remembered in history as Molly Brown. She was born in Hannibal and had a great impact on the world. Few know this is her hometown, too. She did not fit into any of the paths I had created. One night it hit me: who were the women in Hannibal? During my quest I found and used extensive research by Mary Lou Montgomery and Faye Dant, two women who graciously shared their time with me.

Start your walk at North Main and Bird Streets.

DORCAS HAMPTON

Bird Street east of North Main Street

The Robbins store, a few doors east on Bird from North Main, was where Mrs. Kidd's Female Academy was located and where Dorcas met the woman who employed young women as milliners. Hampton lived a difficult life under her cruel and abusive stepmother, which caused her to leave home on her father's Ralls County farm at 14

COURTESY
MARK DENARDIS

and make her way in Hannibal. William Robbins piloted the steamboat that took Dorcas to St. Louis, where she later worked in the galley of a steamboat, although it was a dangerous workplace. Steamboats frequently exploded, killing passengers, but she survived. She tried to find the kind Baker family in Louisville that she had known in childhood, however they were gone. She worked her way back to St. Louis and finally succumbed to the last career afforded a woman then, prostitution. Empowered with financial stability, she eventually moved to Sioux City and opened her own brothel. Her September 1894 court case contesting her father's (John A. Hampton) will was heard in the building that was originally the First Presbyterian Church before becoming the Marion County Courthouse on Fourth Street, a block and a half from Central Park. Dorcas won recognition as his daughter, but was indifferent to the money, as she was already a wealthy woman. In a turn of events, she disinherited her own daughter for eloping just six months after the court case. Her life is chronicled in Mary Lou Montgomery's *The Notorious Madam Shaw*. *maryloumontgomery.com*

Go back to North Main Street and cross it, then continue to Third Street. Turn right on north Third. Arrive at Jim's Journey: The Huck Finn Freedom Center.

JULIA GREELEY

509 North 3rd St.

Born enslaved in Woodland in Marion County, Missouri, Julia became Denver, Colorado's Angel of Charity. Inside Jim's Journey you will see an exhibit sharing Julia's miraculous life. Her trek to St. Louis would have had her pass through Hannibal to board either a steamboat or a train. Working as a domestic after the Civil War,

COURTESY
JULIA GREELEY GUILD

Julia began worshipping in the Catholic Church and carried out a ministry to the poor, carrying a little red wagon through Denver neighborhoods distributing basic survival items that she had collected during her off hours. She has been put forth by the Franciscans to become a saint in the Catholic Church. *juliagreeley.org*

Continue up Third Street and turn left onto Mark Twain Avenue. Turn left onto North Sixth Street and proceed to Denkler Alley.

MARGARET TOBIN BROWN, "The Unsinkable Molly Brown" Molly Brown Home

600 Butler St.

The Unsinkable Molly Brown, a nickname in popular culture given to Margaret Brown by a journalist due to her heroism upon the *Titanic*, was born to Irish immigrants as Margaret Tobin in this modest home on Denkler Alley. Life was hard as Maggie (never called "Molly" before the newspaper article) completed school at 13 and immediately found work stripping tobacco leaves for Garth's Tobacco Company. Proximity to travel happening along the river and the train opened her eyes to opportunity. She moved to Colorado, made her fortune in gold mining, negotiated a union strike in Ludlow, and moved to Newport, where she, then Mrs. J. J. Brown or Margaret Brown, became fast friends with Alva Vanderbilt Belmont, president of the National

COURTESY DECLAN RUTAN; COURTESY MOLLY BROWN HOUSE MUSEUM, DENVER, CO (INSET)

Women's Suffrage Association. There was never a dull moment with the larger-than-life, adventurous Margaret Tobin Brown around. *mollybrown.org*

Return to Mark Twain Avenue and turn left. Directly across from the Hair Co. at 1000 Mark Twain Avenue and up a bit, the store would have been just a few hundred feet off of the current Mark Twain Avenue.

KATE RIDGE

1009 Mark Twain Ave.

Orphaned at the age of five, Kate O'Connell lived with another Irish family and took their surname of Cronin. She became a teacher and traveled during the summers. She married Gus Ridge in 1909 and operated a grocery store. She was raising three children and working while he served in World War I. When he returned he developed the skill of making moonshine whiskey and even did a stint in the Marion County Jail. His career in the Army eventually took him to World War II, after which he divorced Kate. Kate's generosity carried into her death. The ledger she kept of groceries purchased on account read, "Upon my death all these debts are to be forgiven." Her original store is seen here.

COURTESY STEVE CHOU

Continue on Mark Twain Avenue and turn left on Grand Avenue.

MARIE RUOFF BYRUM

808 Grand Ave.

On August 31, 1920, at age 26, she became the first woman to cast her vote in the state of Missouri following the ratification of the 19th Amendment. Voting in a special election to fill a vacancy on the Hannibal City Council, she had

COURTESY GALE RUBLEE

COURTESY LEAGUE OF WOMEN VOTERS OF MISSOURI

apparently joked with her friend Nita Harrison about which one would be the first woman to sign the poll log. Nita was the second woman to vote, just one minute after Marie, at 7:01 a.m. Her father-in-law was the democratic election judge, a local politician, and a cigar maker. I wonder if he handed her one after she voted?

Soon after, her husband Morris King Byrum became city clerk, then auditor and served on the Board of Health. The couple remained active in politics until their move to Florida to retire.

Continue on Grand Avenue, then turn right on Market Street, right on Barton Street, left on Willow Street.

ARIZONA CLEAVER STEMONS

404 Willow St. *(Douglass High School/Arizona Cleaver Park)*

Teacher of French, Director of the commercial business department, and head of the high school department at the segregated Douglass High School, Arizona was a woman with many talents. A founder of the Zetas (Zeta Phi Beta) while attending Howard University, Arizona Cleaver Stemons was a remarkable woman loyal to her hometown and entire community. This marker

ARIZONA LEEDONIA CLEAVER STEMONS
1898-1980

The principal Founder and the First National President of Zeta Phi Beta Sorority, Incorporated was born in Pike County, Missouri. Arizona L. Cleaver graduated from Douglass High School in 1918; after graduation she attended Howard University in Washington, D.C., where she was later approached by Charles Robert Samuel Taylor of Phi Beta Sigma Fraternity, Inc. about forming a sister organization. On January 16, 1920, Zeta Phi Beta, Incorporated was formed and later constitutionally bound as a Sister Organization to the Men of Phi Beta Sigma Fraternity, Inc.

After graduating from Howard University, Miss Cleaver, former Douglassite, returned to Hannibal, Missouri, where she held the positions Director of the Commercial (Business) Department, French instructor, and head of the High School Department for Douglass School.

Arizona Leedonia Cleaver Stemons epitomizes the Sorority's principles of Sisterhood, Scholarship, Service, and Finer Womanhood. As a result of her initial vision, Zeta Phi Beta Sorority, Incorporated is now an international organization that has a membership base of several hundreds of thousands of like-minded women aspiring to uphold the very principles this organization was founded on.

"Zeta now, Zeta tomorrow, Zeta always, should be the thought in the mind of every Zeta woman"
~ Arizona L. Cleaver

COURTESY FAYE DANT, CURATOR JIM'S JOURNEY

was recently placed by her sorority recognizing her fundamental role in their successful organization.

Return to Barton Street, turn right, then left on Market Street, then take a slight right on Lyon Street.

MARY KENNEY O'SULLIVAN
Lyon and 7th Streets

This corner is where Mary Kenney was raised in a row house filled with immigrants new to Hannibal. Recognized nationally as a labor organizer, Mary started as an apprentice dressmaker, then became a book binder. She moved to Chicago and saw the danger, squalor, and abhorrent work conditions in the book binderies. Jane Addams befriended Mary and opened Hull House to the bindery workers. In 1892 Mary assisted Florence Kelley in her investigation of sweatshops and tenements. She was the first woman organizer of the American Federation of Labor, and for the last 20 years of her career she was a factory inspector for the Massachusetts Division of Industrial Safety, eventually a part of the state's Department of Labor and Industries in 1919. She retired in 1934.

Go north on Seventh Street, then left until you reach Eighth Street. Turn right.

LENA MASON
Church Street between 8th and 9th Streets, where the Federal Building parking lot is located

In an era when women evangelists were unknown, Lena Mason was ordained a minister by Hannibal's Allen Chapel African Methodist Episcopal Church. She preached far and wide to audiences both White

and Black. Considered one of the greatest evangelists of her era, the *Kansas City Sun* called her "the world's greatest female evangelist." She even preached to the inmates of the Sedalia, Missouri jail who were skeptical at first but then revived by her message. Politically active, she spoke at the Republican National Convention for the reelection bid of Teddy Roosevelt and at other conventions that allowed women the right to vote. She died in 1924 at the age of 60 having touched tens of thousands of lives with her speaking and her poetry. Her two surviving poems are "A Negro In It" as a response to the 1901 McKinley Assassination and "The Negro in Education."

Continue up Eighth Street, cross Broadway, and turn left on Center Street.

DR. MARGARET SCHMIDT

816 Center St.

Women weren't allowed to earn diplomas from Missouri Medical College, but after auditing courses there, Margaret Schmidt received a medical license from the state of Missouri. She practiced medicine in Hannibal and in those

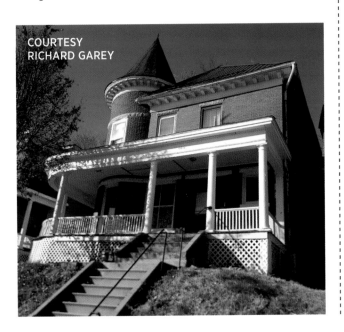

COURTESY RICHARD GAREY

communities she traveled to with her husband, a minister. After Rev. Schmidt's death, Dr. Schmidt lived in this house with daughter, Emily.

Continue east on Center Street (toward the river) and turn left onto Sixth Street.

KATE HELM

419 North 6th St.

Born in Hardin, Kentucky, Kate Park married Cyrus Helm and they moved to Hannibal, where his father was a judge, a contractor, a real estate agent, a railroad director for the Hannibal–St. Joseph Line, and a friend of President

COURTESY DEA HOOVER

Lincoln. She was widowed when he died of typhoid fever. Most likely her father-in-law Judge Helm built this 1869 Italianate-style home to be her new family residence where she would raise her five children alone. Her granddaughter Katherine created the Helm Arts Award given by Hannibal Public Schools.

Head south on Sixth Street/Denkler Alley to Hill Street and turn left on Broadway.

MARY HELM

513 Broadway

The mother of three and the stepmother of five when she arrived in Hannibal with her husband Judge John Helm, she lived a life of caring for her family financially as well as providing

COURTESY STEVE CHOU

their residence. She lived in this home with boarders, servants, and family throughout the years after her husband's death in 1872. She died a woman of means with a house, a barn, and ten acres of property on Palmyra Road in her estate. Her death was two days after the still unsolved, violent murder of Amos Stillwell. Mary's great-great-granddaughters donated part of her wedding trousseau, including a silk walking dress and muff, to the University of Missouri, where the garments are now part of the Department of Textile and Apparel Management in the College of Human Environmental Sciences.

Head toward the river on Broadway.

LILLIAN HERMAN

320 Broadway

Lillian served as Hannibal's first, and so far only, woman to hold the office of mayor. She was willing to fulfill her duties in whatever capacity was necessary, even playing checkers in the July heat. In 1982 Paul Hendrickson wrote a piece for the *Washington Post* about National Tom Sawyer Days 1978 when he attended and witnessed Mayor Herman in Central Park playing against the chamber president in the "Worlds' Largest Checker Game."

COURTESY JIMMY CARTER PRESIDENTIAL LIBRARY AND MUSEUM

He described that day as "swamp hot," which in my recollection is like every 4th of July in Missouri when it's not raining and storming, causing the fireworks to be cancelled. Lillian was appointed city clerk in 1959 after working in the office for two years and continued until she was elected mayor in 1977. She won re-election for a second term, serving until 1981, when she was defeated by her opponent. Then she served as treasurer of the Hannibal Free Public Library Board from 1981–85. She remained lifelong friends with President Jimmy Carter after his visit to Hannibal in 1979, arriving not in a motorcade but very peacefully and smoothly aboard the *Delta Queen* Steamboat.

Continue toward the river on Broadway and turn left onto North Main Street. Head north on Broadway then left on north Fifth Street, then right on Center Street and left onto North Main Street.

HELEN GARTH

201-205 North Main St.

Mrs. Garth was the first woman on the board of directors for the Farmers & Merchants Bank, which was at this location prior to moving to their new building on Broadway. After her husband's death in 1899, she and her daughter donated $25,000 to build a new Hannibal Free Public Library as a memorial to their husband and father, John Garth.

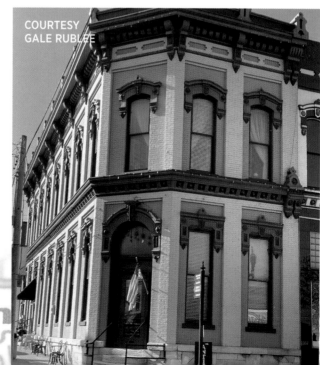

COURTESY GALE RUBLEE

Cemeteries, Caves, and Chaos

Mississippi River

Pleasant Street

Mark Twain Avenue

North 4th Street

North 8th Street

Hill Street

Center Street

Broadway

South Main Street

South 3rd Street

Broadway Extension

Church Street

South 7th Street

South 9th Street

Lyon Street

Market Street

Warren Barrett Drive

Colfax Avenue

Clemens Field

Bluff Street

Riverside Street

Walnut Street

Union Street

Fulton Avenue

State Highway 79

Sodalis Park

Ely Street

Valley Street

Country Road 453

MOUNT OLIVET

Mount Olive Cemetery

Clark Avenue

ROBINSON CEMETERY

Country Road 449

Silvers Lane

Cemeteries, Caves, and Chaos

I have a weakness for alliteration. When trying to forge a path that draws on the lore of Hannibal, this title came to me as one that would convey the challenge that the territory presents. Steep hills, many turns, and spelunking can be found on this walk. Take your time and dress appropriately. You may want to break this up into sections, depending on how much time you can allow. For more cemetery histories: *maryloumontgomery.com*

MARK TWAIN CAVE
Mark Twain Cave & Campground

The cave was initially discovered by Jack Sims. Around 1848, Dr. Joseph Nash McDowell of St. Louis purchased the land including the cave. Inside, he preserved his daughter's body in alcohol in a copper container. He believed her soul, as well as those of his other deceased family members, would not have the same spiritual energy if buried. The town was filled with curiosity about the body, and the sheriff finally made the doctor remove

COURTESY THE MARK TWAIN BOYHOOOD HOME & MUSEUM

her. That entrance to the cave is boarded up today. Making an impression on Mark Twain, it appears in *The Adventures of Tom Sawyer* as McDougal's Cave, where Injun Joe met his demise and where Tom and Becky were lost, as well as in his *Autobiography* and *The Gilded Age*. *marktwaincave.com*

You will see signs for Cameron Cave across from Mark Twain Cave in the same complex.

CAMERON CAVE

You have arrived at another maze, or labyrinth cave, like Mark Twain Cave. A rugged hike with a flashlight is necessary to experience what this cave has to offer. After purchasing tickets at the gift shop, visitors can ride or hike up to the entrance with their cave guide.

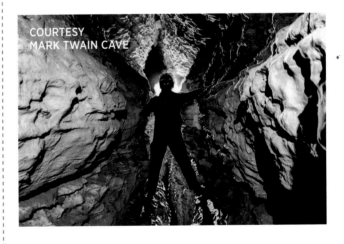

COURTESY MARK TWAIN CAVE

And for the incredibly adventurous and physically fit, consider the Total Eclipse tour that requires crawling and climbing! At the cave but want to be on the outside? Find the three-quarter-mile hiking trail that begins at the left of the Cave Hollow Winery across the street and follow it to return to the opposite side at the end of the trail. Return to the right side of the Winery as you are facing it.

COURTESY MARY LOU MONTGOMERY

Head north back out to MO-79 and turn left onto 79. Turn right onto Riverside Street.

RIVERSIDE CEMETERY

Those interred here reads like a list of Who's Who from the early 1900s of Hannibal including John Cruikshank, Jr., owner of Rockcliffe Mansion, and MLB Hall of Famer Jake Beckley, Pittsburgh Pirates player. David Dubach, who made his fortune in owning flour mills, built his mansion, which is now operated as a bed and breakfast, on Millionaire's Row. The most stunning part of a walk here is the magnificent view from above the river.

Go to the south entrance of Riverside Cemetery to find the entrance gate here.

B'NAI SHOLEM CEMETERY

This Jewish cemetery, deeded in 1871, survives next to Riverside Cemetery. Temple Israel was formed at 1005 Lyon Street in 1935 and closed in 1977 when they merged with Temple B'nai Sholom in Quincy, Illinois. Forced migration and the need to escape the pogroms in Germany in the 1930s led to families making their way to this river town to make a life and a living.

COURTESY GARY W. ELLIOTT

Gary Elliott's book *They Came and They Went: A Brief Account of Hannibal Missouri's Early Jewish Community, and the B'nai Sholem Cemetery (Along With Those Interred There)* gives stories to these touchstones of the past and remember the Jewish community here in Hannibal. One artist interred here is Lester Gaba, who developed lightweight mannequins for the likes of Saks Fifth Avenue.

Head back to MO-79 and turn right. Turn right onto Lover's Leap Road and hike the steep incline. Note: Cars are also allowed up to the overlook with parking.

LOVER'S LEAP

1132 Missouri State Highway 79

The photo with the bridge dates possibly to the early 1940s as the Mark Twain Memorial Bridge was built in 1936. Real photo postcards were very popular in that era. Notice how far out on the cliff the people are in the picture. There were no fences there as there are today and getting

COURTESY DEA HOOVER

this photo was possible ... and I would consider it very dangerous! Once a photo was made it could be placed on a postcard to a friend or loved one to share your travels back home. In 1909 two baseball players showed their skill by catching baseballs dropped from 250 feet above them at the edge of Lover's Leap. Today the area is a beautiful scenic overview that allows you to see the entirety of downtown Hannibal, Mark Twain Memorial Lighthouse, the new Mark Twain Memorial Bridge, the Mark Twain Riverboat, and the beautiful homes up and down the tree-lined streets. I have included the marker telling one of the many versions of the tale of Lover's Leap. As Henry Sweets was looking for this

COURTESY THE MARK TWAIN
BOYHOOD HOME & MUSEUM

photo, we speculated about the origins of the name Lover's Leap, he and I acknowledged that many towns across the US have a Lover's Leap and many different stories abound. It is said that Orion Clemens, Sam's brother, wrote a sensational tale about lovers from differing tribes that was repeated by other newspapers across the country referencing their own high bluffs as the location of the fatality. In my version of the story, I like to think that when they leapt, *she* turned into a bird and saved them both from falling to their deaths and her father was convinced they were meant to be together for eternity. True? I say it's true enough.

Return to 79 and turn right. Once you pass the street that is Washington/Walnut start looking towards the Quarry House on the left. The boarded up entrance is there. Note: In addition to this entrance there is a small cave entrance to the east of the Quarry House, which cavers might have tried to enter during their search.

MURPHY'S CAVE

Birch and Walnut Streets

The Lost Boys of Hannibal were thought to be last seen entering Murphy's Cave. On May 10, 1967, Billy and Joey Hoag and Craig Dowell were seen heading toward their afternoon destination, Murphy's Cave. The highway department was building Highway 79 and the blasting had caused interest in exploring the caves after the crews had completed work each day. If you look up and see the Quarry House, you will find the boarded-up entrance to the cave. The three were seen carrying flashlights and shovels likely looking for adventure like the characters in Mark Twain's novels. They often spent carefree afternoons spelunking in our Cave State. However, a mother of a boy not allowed to go

had said they were going to try the second level of Lover's Leap. (See the marker at Lover's Leap placed by a family member.) After they failed to return home, their parents became alarmed. Search parties commenced. The mystery of their disappearance still lingers. Theories abound that perhaps the blasts had made the rock in the caves unstable and the cave collapsed around them. Recently, a theory has been advanced by three separate psychics that John

COURTESY
GALE RUBLEE

Wayne Gacy was responsible for their disappearance. This theory seems plausible, as he was living in Waterloo, Iowa, and at the time, his mother was in Little Rock, Arkansas, but this has been debunked by the *Lost Boys of Hannibal* podcast, now in its third season of discussion and investigation. The boys may be lost, but they certainly are not forgotten.

Head north on Birch to South Third Street. Go into downtown. Turn right on Bird Street.

LULABELLE'S

111 Bird St.

Built in 1917 by an enterprising madam from Chicago named Sarah Smith, it was not a conversion but was specifically designed and constructed for Smith's intended purpose—complete with an escape stairwell for clients in the rear when law enforcement, or perhaps wives, arrived in the front! Bessie's girls occupied the

COURTESY STEVE CHOU

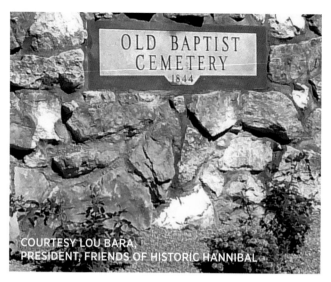

COURTESY LOU BARA,
PRESIDENT, FRIENDS OF HISTORIC HANNIBAL

building after Sarah's untimely death in 1932. The profession was fairly open in the red light district to the point that one of the madams would signal she was open by sweeping the sidewalk in nothing but her shoes. Closed in the mid-1950s when the country took a more conservative swing, it has since been a bed and breakfast and later a restaurant.

Return to North Third Street and turn right. Left onto Mark Twain Avenue. Right onto Hayward Street. Right onto Fairview Street and follow until it becomes north Ann Street. The Cemetery is on your left. Note: a bit of a hilly climb to arrive here.

OLD BAPTIST CEMETERY

Section and Summer Streets

Founded in 1837 by Baptists, it was abandoned by the church due to opposing views on the Civil War. Then anyone could bury their dead without a fee. In 1855 the enslaved Agness Flautleroy was buried with a beautiful headstone provided by her owner, Sophia Hawkins (yes, that Sophia Hawkins, Laura Hawkins's mother). Laura was known to have owned a slave, and there is a marker next to Agness that has Petunia scratched into the marker. There is speculation that the marker may have been placed by Laura for her. Enslaved and free people of color continued to be buried here next to White members of the community, unheard of in the segregated Little Dixie, Missouri, throughout the years. It became the local potter's field as people could be discreetly and anonymously buried in the cover of night without need of paying for a burial. It is the oldest cemetery in town. Many locals had their family members exhumed and moved to Mt. Olivet

Cemetery when it opened. Most notably Mark Twain moved his father and brother Henry. *findagrave.com/cemetery/2231462/old-baptist-cemetery/map*

COURTESY STEVE CHOU

Return to North Ann Street until it becomes Fairview Street. Left onto Hayward Street. Left onto Mark Twain Avenue/Harrison Hill. Right onto Denkler Alley/North Sixth Street.

300 NORTH 6TH ST.

The home of Frank P. Hearne, whose son was implicated but never charged in the 1888 unsolved murder of Amos Stillwell. Stillwell was a victim of an axe murder in his home after attending a party at the Munger House, now home to Labinnah Bistro.

Take North Sixth Street toward Bird Street. Turn right onto Bird Street. Turn left on North Maple Avenue. Right on Broadway. Left on Grand Avenue. Right onto Warren Barrett Drive. Left on Irwin/Patchen Street. Right on Lindell Avenue. Left onto Clark Avenue. Note: This is about a 2-mile walk.

ROBINSON CEMETERY

1200 Clark Ave.

Property outside the city limits was purchased in 1921 by Laura Tate Robinson and her husband Lee Robinson to be platted as a cemetery for people of color. The Robinsons

COURTESY MARY LOU MONTGOMERY

wished to make a place for burials available to people of color, as many cemeteries had restrictions and boards that did not allow non-Whites to be buried. The city annexed the property to bring it inside Hannibal, and it remains in operation today.

North on Clark Avenue toward East Street. Right onto Lindell Avenue. Left onto Irwin/Patchen Street. Left to Lyon Street and turn right onto Lyon. Left onto South Fifth Street. Note: This is about a 2-mile walk.

220 SOUTH 5TH ST.

This indigo blue building has multiple residents listed in the 1923 Hannibal Directory. Most likely a rooming house then, it is a private home now. A more recent owner's daughter has discovered a ghost named Shippa. The home is a highlight on the Haunted Hannibal Tour.

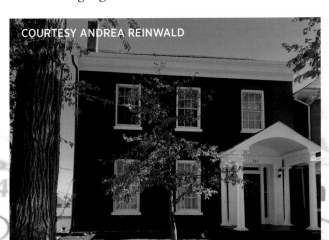

COURTESY ANDREA REINWALD

COURTESY VISIT HANNIBAL

Left onto South Fifth Street. Left onto Lyon Street. Right toward Warren Barrett Drive. Left onto Warren Barrett Drive. Right toward South Third Street and ascend the stairs. Right onto South Third Street. This becomes Birch Street. Right onto Union Street. Right onto Fulton Avenue. Left on State Hwy T. Left onto Bramblett Drive and stay left for another .1 of a mile then right to stay on Bramblett Drive for another .1 miles. Note: This is a 2.1 mile walk.

MT. OLIVET CEMETERY

2340 Fulton Ave.

The final resting place of many of Hannibal's most notable people, including Mark Twain's family. Judge Clemens and Henry Clemens were buried in the Old Baptist Cemetery. Twain was contacted by John Robards to send money to have them moved to Mt. Olivet when it was founded there and his mother and brother would later join them.

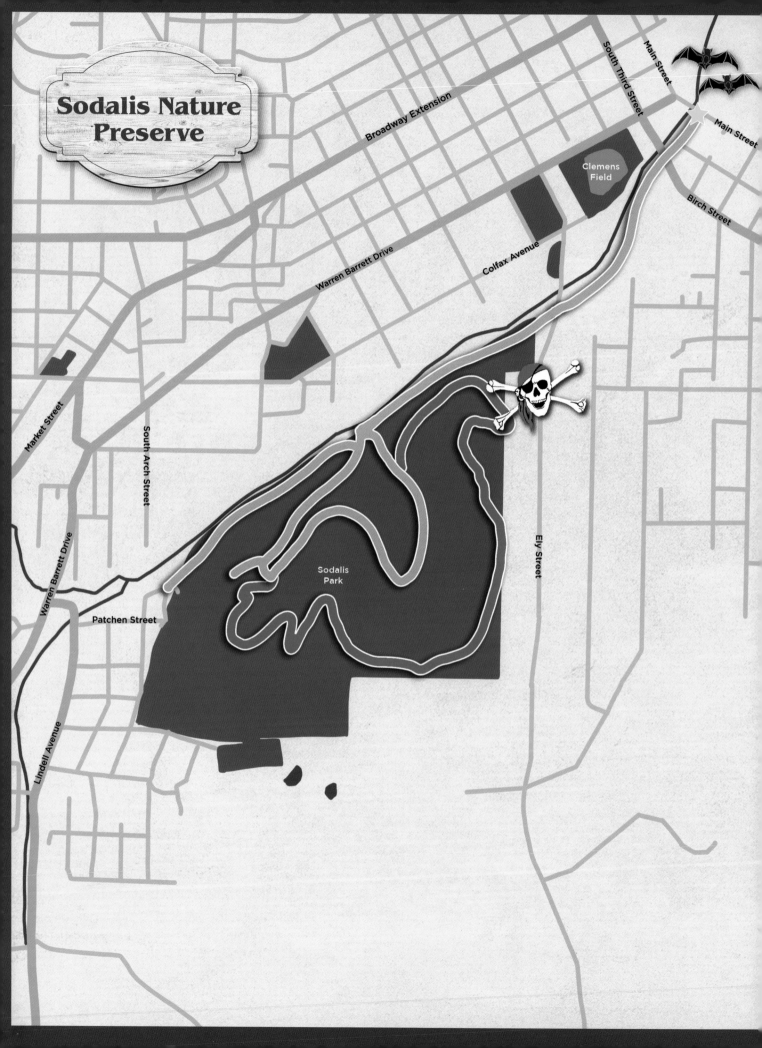

Sodalis Nature Preserve

Broadway Extension

Warren Barrett Drive

Colfax Avenue

Clemens Field

South Third Street

Main Street

Main Street

Birch Street

Market Street

South Arch Street

Ely Street

Warren Barrett Drive

Lindell Avenue

Patchen Street

Sodalis Park

Sodalis Nature Preserve

Why name the preserve Sodalis? To mark the recent discovery of over 211,000 *Myotis sodalis* (*my-oh-tis so-dal-is*) using the lime kiln mine and mine passages as their hibernaculum. Sodalis certainly rolls off the tongue easily and is Latin for "companion" due to the bats forming tightly packed clusters during hibernation. In 1904 the species was found in Indiana and became commonly called the Indiana bat.

Hannibal native Kirsten Alvey-Mudd heads the Missouri Bat Census and played in the area during her childhood. She remembered the bats living there and set up a count in 2012 seeking the Little Brown Bat (*Myotis lucifugus*). She never considered encountering the *Myotis sodalis* colony, believed to live only south of the Missouri River. The deadly white-nose syndrome (WNS) appeared absent in all populations here.

The depth and breadth of the limestone formations made mining quick and easy. The Short Line Railroad leading to St. Louis and the Hannibal–St. Joseph Line heading west gave easy access to transport and sell the lime. The mining process created the additional cave formations. It is theorized that the air movement through the mine system, part of Missouri's Lincoln Fold geologic feature, deters the fungus that causes WNS from thriving. Her discovery of the world's largest Myotis Sodalis population landed on the radar of The Conservation Fund. Their expertise led them to use habitat-mitigation funds designated for the area to purchase the property. Today the Iowa Natural Heritage Foundation holds the conservation easement of the property so that it will remain protected. The Hannibal Parks Department owns and manages the Sodalis Trail.

Prior to creating the preserve, fine lime was piled high across the preserve. Today you see what looks like a sandy beach. The large piles were removed

COURTESY DEA HOOVER

as they were a potential hazard, turning into a quicksand-like substance when wet. The harder you try to get out, the deeper you sink. Those who mapped the mine system wore rope tied around their waists in case they needed to be pulled out of the dangerous mixture when wet. All known entrances into the 26-mile mine system are gated. Only scientists allowed! Outside the openings, in an ongoing citizen science program, Quinton Heaton's students report their annual bat counts to the US Fish and Wildlife Service (USFWS).

Transformed from abandoned limestone quarries into an inviting nature preserve, the now 200-acre preserve attracts visitors of all species. The bats begin arriving from area forests in late summer and practice their mating ritual of creating a swarm prior to entering hibernation in the fall. In the spring they set out to return to their summer homes.

These trails can also be found on the app AllTrails.

About the trails: Main Street trailhead offers wheelchair-accessible parking. The red, blue, and green trails on the Hannibal Parks map are flat. Once you get off the loop, the trail gets hilly.

RR Bridge, Sodalis
Paved Trail
COURTESY DEA HOOVER

SODALIS PAVED TRAIL
(2.7 Miles)

Coming from the Bear Creek Trail you will see the road changes name to Ely. Follow that until you reach the trailhead. If you are driving, aim for 819 Ely St., where you can park. Note: The paved trail is wheelchair accessible. The best place to park is at the trailhead of Bear Creek Trail located at Main and Monroe Streets. This will add .3 miles to the walk along the Paved Trail.

Use the paved trail and refer to the map. Trees have been planted thoughtfully to keep plenty of open space to give insects the space to fly freely.

Look for the path on the sign upon arrival or use the one here in the book.

SITES ALONG THE WAY ARE:

- **RAILROAD BRIDGE**
- **COTTONWOOD TREE:** You will see bittersweet along the trail. It begins yellow and turns pink to red.
- **QUEEN ANNE'S LACE:** (also known as wild carrot) is plentiful here.
- **LIME KILN:** This area still has the "sandy beaches" from the lime mining that took place prior to clean up. The spots of white along the ground are remnants of this big industry in Hannibal.
- **SCOURING RUSH:** Hollow inside and makes a great whistle!

Cottonwood Tree

Bittersweet

Sandy Beach Lime

Bittersweet

Lime along the trail

Queen Anne's Lace

Scouring Rush

ALL PHOTOS COURTESY DEA HOOVER

Bat Cluster
COURTESY
GALE RUBLEE

BBQ Pit
COURTESY
DEA HOOVER

GATES 23 and **24** are chute gates. In order for the bats to get enough lift to fly, they need to be elevated on departure, as the ground does not drop off near the mine entrance.

There is a distinct temperature difference inside the cave, and you often feel the air leaving the caves. If it is warm then it feels cooler, and if it is cool it feels warmer.

Gate 24
COURTESY
DEA HOOVER

Bear Creek
COURTESY
DEA HOOVER

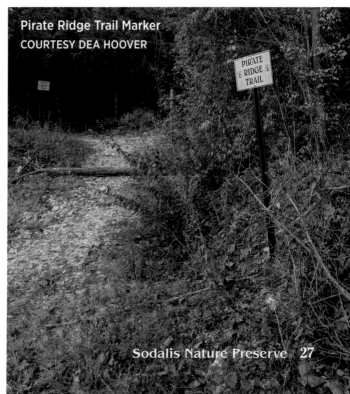

Pirate Ridge Trail Marker
COURTESY DEA HOOVER

PIRATE RIDGE TRAIL
(2 Miles)

This road was originally a track. ATVs ran along it prior to the designation as a preserve. You will see some signage and unpaved walkways as you continue around on the trail. This trail is steep, and you may wish to bring a walking stick.

Gardens and Parks Walk

I-72 | US-36 | MO-110

Mississippi River

Bridge Street

Cardiff Drive

Mark Twain Avenue

Grand Avenue

North Street

North 1st Street

North Main Street

North 3rd Street

North 4th Street

North 5th Street

North 6th Street

North 7th Street

Hill Street

Bird Street

Center Street

Broadway Extension

Church Street

Lyon Street

South 4th Street

South 5th Street

South 6th Street

South 7th Street

South Main Str

Clemens Field

Birch Street

Grand Avenue

Broadway Extension

Warren Barrett Drive

Colfax Avenue

Market Street

Ely Street

Sodalis Park

Gardens and Parks Walk

If you choose to tackle the entire walk at once, you will clock approximately six miles. Once you arrive in the parks, you will want to do additional walking to explore. You may wish to drive to the parks, as there are scenic hikes upon arrival. Hannibal has a wonderful parks department that has created useful content found on its website, along with event information. To see all of the parks, visit: *hannibalparks.org*. The site also shows updates about any sections of parks that may be washed out or have obstructions. The parks department strives to bring out the best in all of Hannibal's public parks and green spaces.

NIPPER PARK
103 Broadway

Named for Ainsworth N. Nipper, superintendent of the Board of Public Works and Electric Light and Water Department, it offers a lovely view of the river and newly refurbished marina. Located in Glascock Landing, you may see a passenger riverboat vessel resembling a paddlewheeler of old or a sleek, new riverboat docked here. There is a half-mile walking path and easy access to the marina. The area is level and can accommodate any wheeled assistance devices making it accessible to all.

Follow the walking path north to where it ends on Hill Street. Turn left on Hill, then right on First Street, which then becomes Bridge Street. Walk north under the bridge until you see Wabash Avenue. Take Wabash to Konder Trail, which will lead you into the park.

Glascock Landing, where Nipper Park is located
COURTESY DEA HOOVER

COURTESY
LIBRARY OF CONGRESS

If you are driving: Consider parking on Wabash, walking all the paths, then retracing your steps back to your car.

Upon arrival or when near Riverview Park, you may want to use the AllTrails app. It shows the trails within parks all over the country, and it features Riverview Park here in Hannibal.

- -

RIVERVIEW PARK
2000 Harrison Hill

Riverview Park is 465 acres. City philanthropist and lumber baron W. B. Pettibone donated 450 acres and purchased the adjoining properties to protect the view and prevent encroachment from development. Listed on the National Register of Historic Places in 2005, it boasts a statue of Mark Twain peering down over the Mississippi River. Pettibone employed Ossian C. Simonds, garden architect for Rockcliffe Mansion, to design the park as a welcoming place for carriage

COURTESY
GALE RUBLEE

riding and for pedestrians. The Prairie Style design is for passive enjoyment, thus no picnic facilities, playgrounds, or sports fields. The marker placed in 1926 honoring Pettibone for his gift is Vermont granite. Here are a few trees that you may encounter: black cherry, pawpaw, black walnut, hackberry, basswood, shagbark hickory, Kentucky coffeetree, and sassafras. An inventory in 2005 noted these species. However, storms and disease take their toll every season.

COURTESY DOUG WALLICK

Follow Riverview Park Road to Harrison Hill and turn left. Then a quick left on Section Street, which will jog right and become Pleasant Street. Left on North Sixth Street. Right on Summer Street. Left on Angle Street. Right onto Cardiff Drive.

BECKY'S BUTTERFLY GARDEN AT CARDIFF HILL OVERLOOK

Founded in 2004 by a Girl Scout troop earning their badges, the garden is now being maintained by the Mississippi Hills Chapter of Missouri Master Naturalists in conjunction with a local Girl Scout troop. A breathtaking view combines with the beauty of Missouri's native plants. Check out the sign to learn about local pollinators.

Find information on the Missouri Master Naturalist Program here: *extension.missouri.edu/ programs/missouri-master-naturalist.*

- -

Continue heading down on Cardiff Drive.

PRIVATE NATIVE GARDEN
208 Cardiff Dr.

Kristy Trevathan graciously offers a view of her native garden. This street meanders down the bluff and gives you the feeling of being far away from the bustle of daily life. The views are spectacular, and it's a beautiful walk or drive. See what she has growing today!

COURTESY
KRISTY TREVATHAN

Continue down Cardiff Drive. Turn left on Rock Street.

5 MARK TWAIN MEMORIAL LIGHTHOUSE

East Rock Street

This is the second memorial lighthouse, as the first one, built 1935, was leveled in a storm in 1960. Rebuilt three years later, it stood until the third and current lighthouse was built for the Hannibal 2019 Bicentennial. Never used as an actual lighthouse, as it is too far inland, it commemorates the massive river traffic during the boom times of the steamboat and lumber eras. Today barge traffic is still heavy coming from Minnesota down to New Orleans. Since locks are required to pass through channels above Alton, not more than a 15-barge tow will be seen here. One barge equals the capacity of over 60 tractor trailers, an efficient mode of

COURTESY
DAVE AND PAULA HIRNER -
FLYING SQUIRREL AERIAL OPTICS

transportation when the destination is located along the river. Be sure to read the storyboard and get photos from this view. Note that there are two levels.

Directions if you take the 244 steps down: Take Rock Street to Mark Twain Avenue/Third Street and follow Third to North Street. Take a right on North and a left on North Fifth Street until you arrive at Central Park.

6 CENTRAL PARK

North 4th and Center Streets

A gift of land from Stephen Glascock in 1836 has now become today's one-acre Central Park. Glascock replatted the city after founder Moses Bates laid out the initial grid pattern. By declaring that this acre of ground was strictly for the benefit of the citizens, it did not become the site of the courthouse, as in many other town squares. Although Palmyra is the county seat of Marion, there is also a courthouse

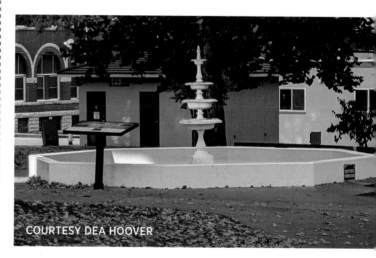

COURTESY DEA HOOVER

in Hannibal. Initially a court of common pleas was built in Hannibal to serve the river traffic; it quickly expanded to offer other court services. Many events important to Hannibal have happened in the park, such as the Chautauqua gatherings in the early 1900s, the Union Army setting up camp during the Civil War, and the First Regimental Band performing throughout the summers.

Note the stone placed on the northwest corner of the park across from Fifth St. Baptist Church, designating Hannibal's first schoolhouse, a log cabin built in 1830. A wonderful storyboard installed for the bicentennial shares the story of Central Park. You will see the statue of Henry Hatch, representative to the US Congress, who passed the act funding land-grant colleges to accommodate agricultural experimentation. It carries his name as the Hatch Act of 1817. Importantly for the town, he sponsored the authorization of the Federal Building and US Post Office at 600 Broadway. A popular event location during the National Tom Sawyer Days over the 4th of July, it also offers a weekly Farmers Market from the end of April through October near Fifth and Broadway that features only local growers. The fountain offers a focal point and welcome place of respite in the center of the park.

Head east on Broadway until you see Third Street. Look on the even number address side.

BROADWAY NATIVE GARDEN
220 Broadway
Peek between the buildings to enjoy this native shrub garden off to the side from all the activity on Broadway.

COURTESY
KRISTY TREVATHAN

Continue east on Broadway and make a left on North Main and a right on Bird Street.

KRISTY'S GARDEN
Bird and North Main Streets on the east side of the street
This private property brings beauty to the heart of downtown Hannibal. All native plants can be found here no matter what season of the year.

COURTESY
KRISTY TREVATHAN

Return to Main Street. Take a left on North Third Street. Cross over Warren Barrett Drive. You will see signs pointing to Clemens Field right next door.

ADMIRAL COONTZ RECREATION CENTER
301 Warren Barrett Dr.
The newly named recreation center is the old armory. Soon, a transom from the USS *Coontz*, a guided missile frigate named for Hannibal native Admiral Robert E. Coontz, will be placed in

COURTESY GALE RUBLEE

front of this building named in his honor. Coontz was born in 1864 and was appointed to the Naval Academy by Rep. William Hatch. Six thousand people attended his funeral, and Governor Guy Park served as an honorary pallbearer. He is buried with family in Mt. Olivet Cemetery. He wrote an autobiography, *From the Mississippi to the Sea*, and followed it up with *True Anecdotes of an Admiral*. Another success story from this tiny river town.

- -

Head east on Warren Barrett Drive and turn right on South Main Street. There you will come to the path called Bear Creek Trail. You can take the 3.5-mile walk to the Sodalis Nature Preserve.

HEAD OF BEAR CREEK TRAIL

Near 450 South Main St.

Once you arrive at the entrance to the Bear Creek Trail, you can take a relaxing walk along the creek that was once known as the Hannibal River. Antoine Soulard named many areas he surveyed after the Carthaginians, and this river was no exception. As time progressed, the name for the town became Hannibal, taken from this river. Then the river name went back to the name christened by the first White man to enter the territory, a Belgian monk named Louis Hennepin. He named the area for the number of

bears making their habitat along the waterway. As you progress across Warren Barrett Drive you will arrive at the latest addition to Hannibal's park system, Sodalis Nature Preserve. Go to the previous walk for details on this wonderful exploration of a recently discovered home of Indiana bats!

COURTESY GALE RUBLEE

Mural Walk

Mississippi
River

Glascock's
Landing

Hill Street

North 3rd Street

North 4th Street

North 1st Street

North Main Street

Center Street

Broadway

Central
Park

Broadway Extension

South 3rd Street

South 4th Street

South 5th Street

Church Street

Lyon Street

South Main Street

Birch Street

EAGLE EYE BECKLEY

Jacob Peter "Eagle Eye" Beckley
was born in Hannibal in 1867. He
played professional baseball from
1888 to 1907. To this day, Beckley
holds the MLB record for put outs
with 23,767 and ranks fourth with
244 triples. Even though early in
the New York Giants, Pittsburgh
Pirates, and Cincinnati Reds, he
was inducted to the Professional
Baseball Hall of Fame in 1971.

Karlock's Kars

Mural Walk

I'm proud to show you some great art by local northern Missouri boys. Bob Allen is a local artist who began his career painting vehicle pinstripes and advertising on glass windows and buildings for businesses. In his retirement he has found joy in creating long-lasting ghost murals in Hannibal. An article by Trevor McDonald in the *Courier-Post* stated that the project began as a conversation he had with Mark Twain reenactor Jim Waddell about ideas to celebrate Hannibal's bicentennial. I contacted him about his murals around town and was excited to learn that Bob actually grew up in my hometown of Vandalia, Missouri, and knows some of my family. When I picked up the phone to call him, I didn't expect that connection! He said that the depictions of businesses of days gone by interested him and that he appreciates the largesse of the building owners who allow him to paint signs not necessarily advertising their own goods.

In mural paintings of the past, muted colors were mixed with varnish and consequently do not fade nearly as quickly as bright colors. Faded signs on brick from days gone by are ghosts of the original murals. When Allen creates a ghost mural, he uses multiple layers of paint to give the appearance of a somewhat time-worn ad with neutral color. Self-taught and always learning, he is very modest about the final products of ghost and current advertising murals.

Anthony Billups now resides in Nashville pursuing his career as an artist and a musician. He asked Olasubomi Bashorun to join in the creativity. You will see a series of historic figures by these two.

COURTESY DEA HOOVER

Start at South Main and Church Streets, look west and you will see this mural in the parking lot.

KARLOCK'S KARS
Main and Church Streets in parking lot, wall facing east

A mural for a museum of pop culture, specifically cars, pops with color unlike the other murals. Commissioned to show the inside out, this mural will have you wanting to see inside this 1860 building!

Continue west on Church Street and turn right onto Fourth Street. Look to your left as you approach Broadway.

BIG MUDDY BBQ
401 Broadway

Moved out to the highway, this original location of Big Muddy has become a recent ghost mural, as the business no longer resides there. The vibrant colors on the building let the spectator know it was painted recently by Bob for the owners to attract business as people drive along Broadway. The Missouri River has always been

COURTESY DEA HOOVER

known as the Big Muddy, and Mark Twain wrote about the danger and difficulty of navigating along the quickly changing river. A very skilled steamboat captain was required to safely transport cargo and people. A shining example of the difficulty of the river is showcased at The Steamboat Arabia Museum in Kansas City, home to a steamboat exhumed from a corn field rather than the current river bed due to the Missouri's unpredictable change of course through the years.

Right on Broadway, then left on North Third Street. Look up as you approach Center Street

DIAMOND JO LINE STEAMERS
120 North 3rd St.
A flyer from 1910 shows this steamer line transported passengers on the *Grey Eagle* from Quincy, Illinois, to Hannibal, Missouri, to Louisiana, Missouri, to Clarksville, Missouri, for $1. That is equivalent to about $30 in 2022 and works out to about two weeks of wages for a union baker or boilermaker at the time working a 50-hour week. Their boats ran trips to Quincy and Hannibal throughout the day. The Diamond Jo line was purchased in 1911 by Streckfus Lines out of St. Louis, the same company that built the SS *Admiral* in 1940 out of steel. I had cruised on the *Admiral* as a graduation event for students from Washington University in St. Louis in 1992. I was headed downtown to meet a tour group along the riverfront and stumbled onto it being dismantled in 2011. My in-laws were in town from New Jersey and we took them to the riverfront to see the end of an era with others who had fond memories.

Streckfus had seen the future for steamboats when the railroads came along. He knew that the majority of freight would be carried by rail and that tourism and entertainment excursions were the wave of the

future. He removed staterooms, as the Diamond Jo offered many long-term cruises from St. Paul to St. Louis before the turn of the century, and installed dance floors so 2,000 people could board the vessel and enjoy music and fun. Passengers enjoyed picnics and moonlight cruises for dancing the night away. Think of the excitement this held for people in these

COURTESY DEA HOOVER

small towns along and near the river—they could board and experience entertainment that otherwise would have bypassed their local opera houses.

Take a right on Center Street and cross Main Street. Look in the alley behind the Hannibal Haunted Ghost Tours lot on the white wall.

EAGLE EYE BECKLEY
White wall on Whistle Stop Café building
Take a look at Major League Baseball history as you see this depiction of Eagle Eye Beckley by Anthony Billups and Olasubomi Bashorun. Born here in Hannibal, Hall of Famer Jacob Peter Beckley had a few plays on the field that would not be allowed today. One was the hidden-ball trick, in which he had a second baseball tucked in his uniform or under the bag, that he would throw to an outfielder. When the

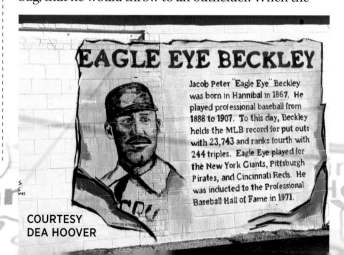

EAGLE EYE BECKLEY

Jacob Peter "Eagle Eye" Beckley was born in Hannibal in 1867. He played professional baseball from 1888 to 1907. To this day, Beckley holds the MLB record for put outs with 23,743 and ranks fourth with 244 triples. Eagle Eye played for the New York Giants, Pittsburgh Pirates, and Cincinnati Reds. He was inducted to the Professional Baseball Hall of Fame in 1971.

COURTESY DEA HOOVER

COURTESY DEA HOOVER

runner on first ran to second, he threw the game ball to the second baseman, who would tag the runner out. When Honus Wagner played for Louisville he fell prey to this tactic. Another play that helped Beckley's batting average was his ability to bunt with the handle, or small end of the bat. He was one of only three players in the league to sport facial hair, in his case a long mustache. When he was earning his nickname "Eagle Eye" for his amazing hitting ability, Beckley sometimes yelled "Chickazoola!" to suck the confidence out of opposing pitchers. He played for the Reds, Pirates, Cardinals, and eventually returned to Hannibal in 1911 to bat and manage a semi-pro team. He then retired and got into the grain business. A company in Cincinnati that he placed a grain order with sent a cable saying, "We can't find you in Dun and Bradstreet." Beckley replied, "Look in Spalding Baseball Guide for any of the last 20 years." He is buried in Riverside Cemetery here in town.

Return to North Main, cross Bird Street, and start looking up and to the right.

WOMEN'S SHOES
308 North Main St.
Carol Cox commissioned Allen to create this mural about ladies' shoes from a bygone era. She had a framed sign of the ad inside her building and asked for it to be recreated

on the brick wall outside her building. He took some artistic license. The sign directs people to 304 North Main Street for women's shoes.

Cross to the other side of North Main Street and continue north. Look up on the wall past the Old Dutch General Store.

BEAR CREEK LIME CO.
323 North Main St.
Allen's first ghost sign depicts one of the top natural resources found along the Lincoln Fold, as it's named in geological terms. Limestone has been generously formed and deposited all along the Mississippi River bluffs. Bear Creek was the name given by early explorers before Antoine Soulard mapped it as the Hannibal River. The name Bear Creek literally meant that bears were frequently seen fishing along the waterway. The quarrying of limestone and mining of pharmaceutical grade lime were big businesses along with steamboating and lumber. However, the limestone mining continues today. From 1920 to 2008 a Missouri Department of Natural Resources study showed that 94 of Missouri's 114 counties quarried limestone with 3.6 billion short tons of limestone worth $24.1 billion at current prices.

COURTESY DEA HOOVER

The view from Cardiff Hill
COURTESY DEA HOOVER

Afterword

I first met Josh Stevens, owner of Reedy Press, in 2019 when we were introduced by Nancy Milton. She believed we could support each other's goals in business and she was right. Our first foray was creating actual tours for Reedy guidebooks of the St. Louis area. In February of 2020, I worked with Carolyn Mueller, the author of the inaugural book in this walking tour series, *Forest Park: A Walk through History*, to create and offer walking tours with trained guides centered around one of the walks in her book. We launched the tours in March 2020 and ran a few before the pandemic shutdown occurred. Then everything stopped for all of us.

I received a phone call in May from Josh asking how our business was doing. After a sigh, I responded, "About like you'd expect." I own two tour companies and had just refunded most of the till, then my husband, and partner in the business, had continued health problems that were going to need to be addressed during the summer. Josh casually tossed out the offer for me to become an author and write a walking tour book to add to the series. I immediately suggested Hannibal, most likely not what he thought would be my suggestion as a local St. Louis tour guide. But Hannibal is where it all started for me, and I wanted to return to it in this way.

Throughout my career as a tour director, I realized what a big deal it is to be connected to Mark Twain's childhood home, now firmly placed in everyone's vernacular as America's Hometown. The Hannibal Visitors phone number has been 1-TOM-AND-HUCK for years.

I hope that you enjoyed the brief tour of this historic town that is continuing into the future with committed citizens who embrace its beauty, history, and potential. I hope you are curious and research some of the subject matter more deeply using the Sources section, and that you visit the Mark Twain Boyhood Home and Museum, Jim's Journey, and the Hannibal History Museum, and go rollin' on the river. Captain Steve and Sandy will show you a good time!

COURTESY DAVE AND PAULA HIRNER - FLYING SQUIRREL AERIAL OPTICS

Sources

Allen, Bob, muralist

Blake, Nicole, author. *mylillianherman.blogspot.com*

Bradley, John H., "Stratigraphy of the Kimmswick Limestone of Missouri and Illinois," *The Journal of Geology*, vol. 33, no. 1 (1925): 49–74, *jstor.org/stable/30059170*

britannica.com/biography/Mary-Kenney-OSullivan

Chou, Steve, keeper of the photos and author. *shop.shsmo.org/hannibal-the-otis-howell-collection-by-steve-chou*

conservationfund.org/projects/sodalis-nature-preserve

courant.com/sdut-new-preserve-in-missouri-aims-to-protect-2015dec20-story

Creason, Nora, Laura Hawkins Frazer House

Dant, Faye, Executive Director at Jim's Journey: Huck Finn Freedom Center

dnr.mo.gov/document-search/limestone-pub2902/pub2902 extension.missouri.edu/publications/ued6063

Findagrave.com

fraser.stlouisfed.org/title/union-scale-wages-hours-labor-3912/union-scale-wages-hours-labor-1907-1912-476865?start_page=68

Garey, Richard, Twain reenactor and historian

Hamilton, Esley, facilitated placing on National Register of Historic Places

Hannibal Courier-Post via HFPL

Hannibal Free Public Library

hannibal.net/archive/article/latest-ghost-sign-brings-history-to-life/article_6a3db351-6a9c-5036-a736-092749e8586b

hannibalparks.org/parks/sodalis-nature-preserve

Haunted Hannibal Tour

Hirner, Dave and Paula. Flying Squirrel Aerial Optics. *www.flyingsquirrelao.com*

Jimmy Carter Presidential Library

lindenwood.edu/files/resources/the-confluence-spring-summer-2012-ritter.pdf

Marks, Ken and Lisa, authors, *Haunted Hannibal*

Metcalf, Don, Laura Frazier Hawkins House

mollybrown.org/about-molly-brown

momarion.genealogyvillage.com/history/marionimg

Montgomery, Mary Lou, writer, researcher, genealogist, and former *Hannibal Courier-Post* editor. *Maryloumontgomery.com*

mostateparks.com/sites/mostateparks/files/Central%20 Park%20HD.pdf

mostateparks.com/sites/mostateparks/files/Federal%20 Bldg.pdf

Ober, Patrick K., "The Body in the Cave: Dr. Joseph McDowell's Influence on Mark Twain," *Mark Twain Journal*, vol. 41, no. 2 (2003): 4–15, *jstor.org/stable/41641534*

Rapp, Megan, Visit Hannibal, *visithannibal.com*

Rublee, Gale, local guide

sabr.org/bioproj/person/jake-beckley

Silver, Hallie Yundt, Hannibal Free Public Library Director and connector to Steve Chou

steamboats.com/museum/davet-illustrationsdiamondjo

Sweets, Henry, The Mark Twain Boyhood Home & Museum curator

Terry, Captain Steve and Sandy, *marktwainriverboat.com*

TheClio.com

tn.gov/twra/wildlife/mammals/mammals-bats/indiana-bat-myotis

uscourts.gov/educational-resources/educational-activities/ facts-and-case-summary-gideon-v-wainwright

waterwaysjournal.net/2018/03/26/hannibal-asks-corps-for-riverfront-renovations

washingtonpost.com/archive/lifestyle/1982/07/04/life-on-the-mississippi/1f48e518-5f40-4a71-a0d0-d067a6f55fe4

whig.com/archive/article/elegance-of-steamboat-mary/ article_a3f8a8d6-5bc4-5917-9459-bbc2dec48d53

Index

Index